T0131468

Archway Publishing books may be ordered through booksellers or by contacting:

Archway Publishing
1663 Liberty Drive
Bloomington, IN 47403
www.archwaypublishing.com
844-669-3957

Interior Image Credit: Mahnoor Ali

ISBN: 978-1-6657-0883-8 (sc)
ISBN: 978-1-6657-0884-5 (e)

Print information available on the last page.

Archway Publishing rev. date: 07/08/2021

I hear my mother's voice saying Isabella, Isabella it's time to get up for school sweet heart. As I am awakened to get up for school, I cannot help but feel anxious, excited and nervous. It is the first day of school and I will be starting the second grade I can only imagine all the wonderful things that will happen on this day. There are so many thoughts racing through my mind, I decided to get on my knees and pray for a wonderful first day. I began to speak saying only if heaven knew how I want this school year to be better than last year, I want to have a great teacher and friends.

My mother bought me a beautiful floral dress to wear, for the first day of school, so I was filled with joy as I looked upon my reflection in the mirror. I head out to school when I arrived, my teacher whose name is Mrs. Smith seems to be very sweet and I noticed some of my friends from first grade, in my mind I was like wow this school year is going to be great!

The first assignment was given, Mrs. Smith wanted each of us to write about our summer vacation. I began writing about my adventure to Walt Disney World and how I loved the racing cars. When the teacher approached my desk she said Isabella, oh my what a messy handwriting you have Isabella. Oh, no my smile quickly became a frown, ugh I said to myself I do not write as good as the other students, and I was no longer happy about sharing my summer vacation with the class. Now it is time for lunch they are having my favorite pizza, corn and toss salad. I talked to two of my friends from first grade Emma and Sophia boy was I happy to see them! Right after lunch it is recess we are about to play kickball, now we are about to pick teams, as the names were being called my name was never called, Jesse yelled out saying Isabella no one wants to play with you because your skin is to dark and you are too big! As I walked away I said to myself oh boy only if he knew how bad his words hurt me, I began to pray only if heaven knew how mean the kids were to me? I just wanted to play, I wanted friends!

It is the next day of school we are at gym, I was jump roping with Emma and Sophia, I overheard Emma say to Sophia ask Isabella who is her best friend? I said Sophia it does not take a rocket science to know that Emma is my best friend. I walked over to the water fountain I overheard Emma say Isabella is not my best friend, matter of fact I don't even like her at all. I went to Emma and said I heard you that is not a nice thing to say, you must be careful of other people feelings. School has now ended I went home to talk with my mom, about how school was going at the dinner table; I said mom I really need to talk to you? she replied not now Isabella I am talking with your sister about cheerleading.

Wow! I am really crushed my mom does not have time for me, so I go to my room and I cry and my pillow is soaked with tears. I yelled out loud saying only if heaven knew the pain I was feeling, my self-esteem is low, the teacher is not nice, I do not have any friends, no one wants to be around or play with me; What is wrong with "I" Isabella heaven? I cried more than I have ever cried. Another day at school everything is still the same, I became so angry with how everyone treated me until I started being mean to others. Hmmm, it must be something better I do not want school to be like this and I want to be a better me. After school, it was the same routine, homework, dinner, chores and then bed. On this night before I went to sleep, I got on my knees to say my prayer but this time it was different.

I cried out loud and said only if heaven knew that I am angry, I am becoming a bully, only if heaven knew that I feel so alone not only at school but even with my family. Only if heaven could feel my pain of loneliness; I said heaven please make me over again, teach me how to embrace my dark skin, and to love my self unconditionally because I am fearfully and wonderfully made. Miraculously, on the next day of school, it was something different about this particular day, it was bright, school was incredible my teacher complimented my handwriting, no one bullied me, I was picked for kickball, Emma and Sophia was so nice. I made it home from school to my surprise my mom said Isabella how was school? I was excited to tell her about my great day.

Today could have not been more of a perfect day, I finally look forward to the rest of the school year. As, I prayed tonight I exclaimed with excitement saying "Heaven you have heard me all alone, I thank you for answering me". You are awesome! Thanks for loving me Isabella!

If only heaven knew!

End

Printed in the United States
by Baker & Taylor Publisher Services